Drumbo Ontario and Area in Photos, Saving Our History One Photo at a Time

Photography
by Barbara Raué
2012

Series Name:
Cruising Ontario

Book 13: Drumbo

Cover photo: House c. 1880

Series Name: Cruising Ontario

Other Books by Barbara Raue

Coins and Gems

Arrows, Indians and Love

The Life and Times of Barbara
Volume 1: Inventions That Have Enhanced My Life
Volume 2: Entertainment That I Have Enjoyed
Volume 3: East Coast Trips
Volume 4: Olympics
Volume 5: Wonders of the World

Drumbo and Area

Drumbo - formerly Muma Corners, acquired its name in 1852. It is said that the meaning of the word is "a hump backed cow". The community was named after Drumbo, Ireland. It is located in Blandford-Blenheim Township, Oxford County at the crossroads of County Road #3 (Wilmot Street) and County Road #29 (Oxford Street); this is south of the 401 Highway and 24 kilometres northeast of Woodstock.

Princeton is located in Oxford County on Country Road #3, 22 kilometres east of Woodstock.

Plattsville is located on Township Road 13 & 42 (Albert Street) and Regional Road 8. It is located north of Highway 401 and 32 kilometres northeast of Woodstock. The community was named for its founder, Edward Platt, who settled in 1811 and built a flour mill.

Washington is on County Road 3 (Washington Road) and Regional Road 8, east of Plattsville.

Windfall is located on Oxford Road 29, north of Highway 401, west of Drumbo.

Drumbo

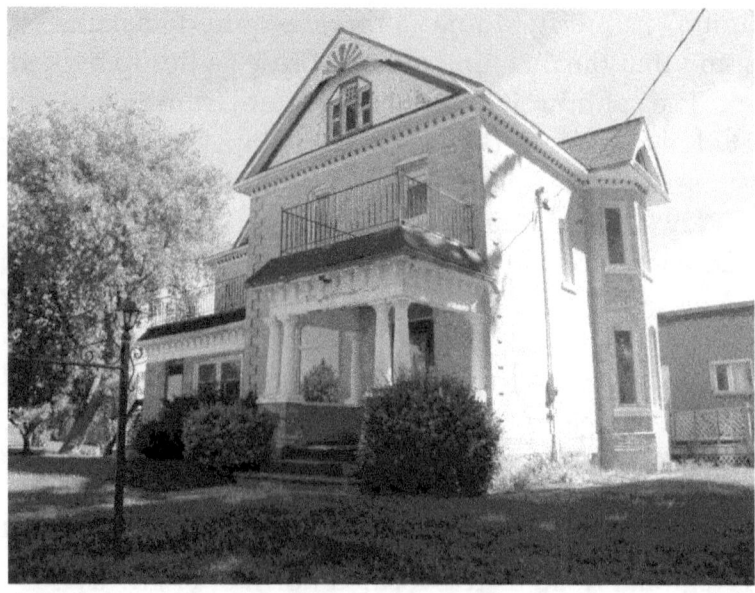

Yellow brick, Ionic style pillars supporting an upper balcony

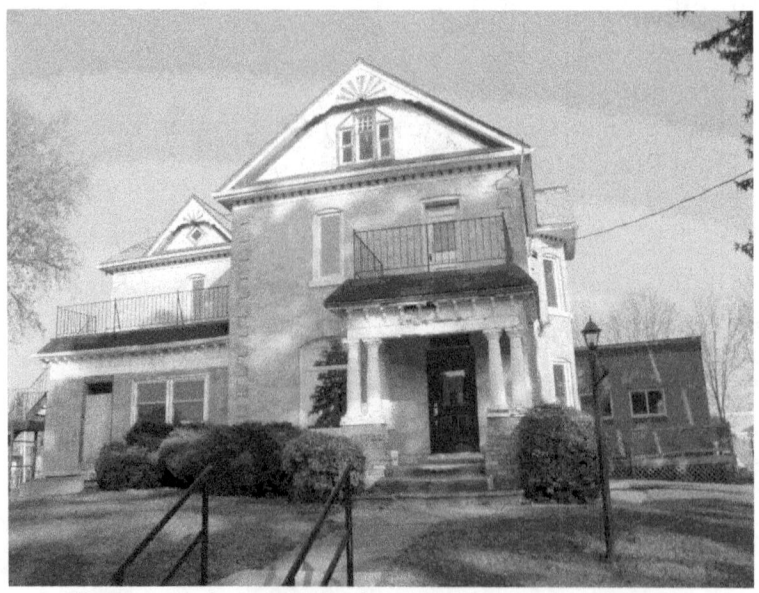

Decorated centre arch – Gothic Revival style

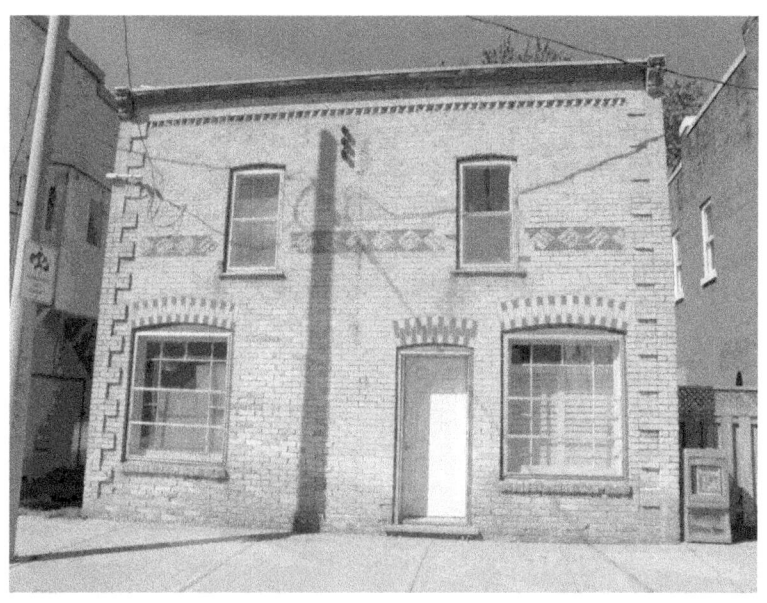

Dichromatic brickwork with two colours of brick for decoration

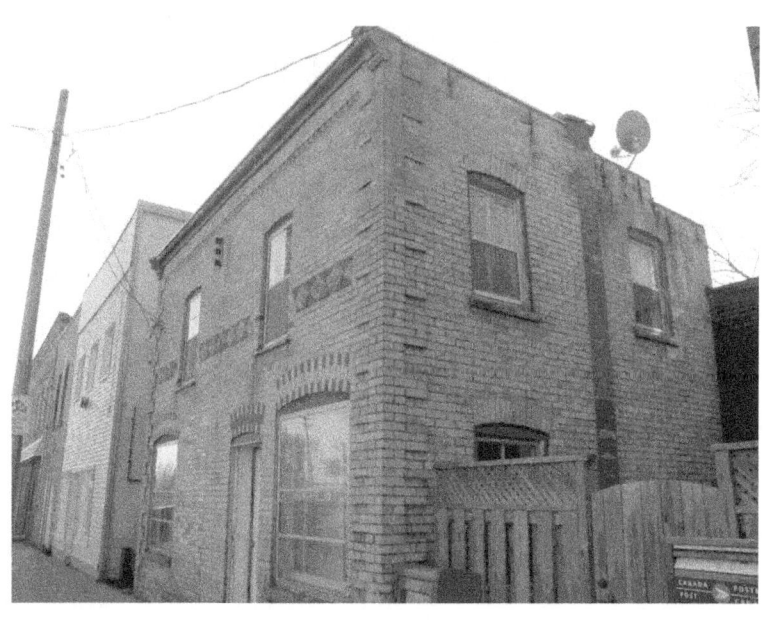

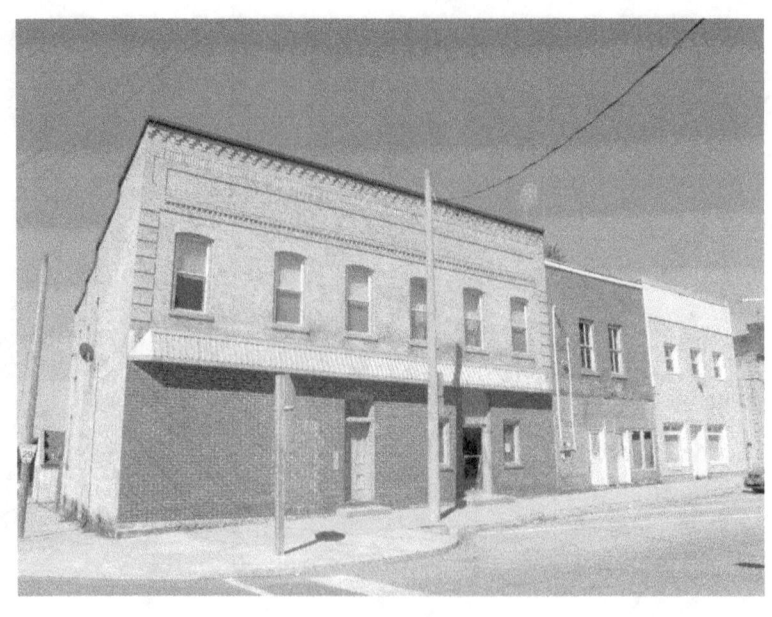

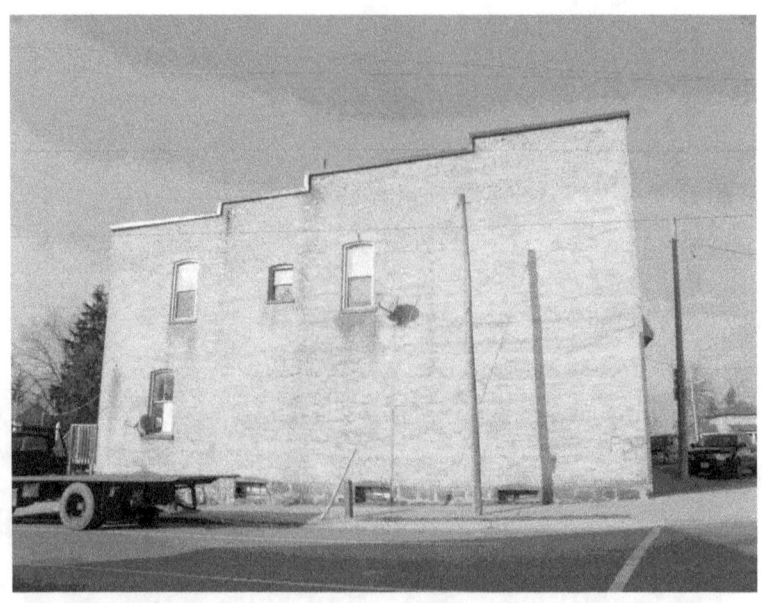

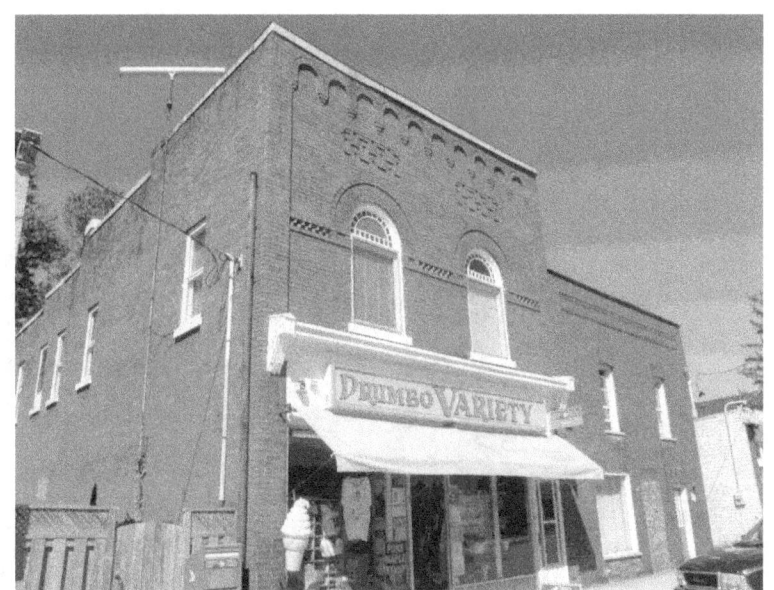

Renaissance Revival storefront

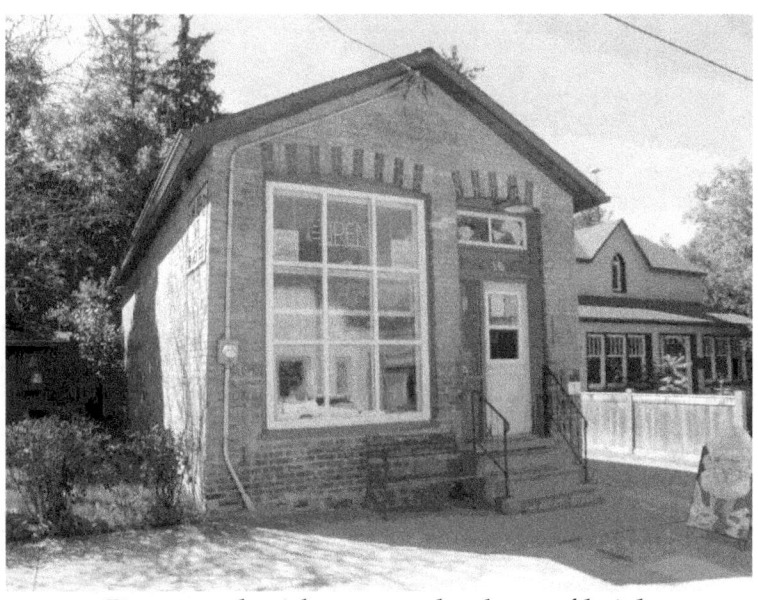

Decorated with a second colour of brick
#16

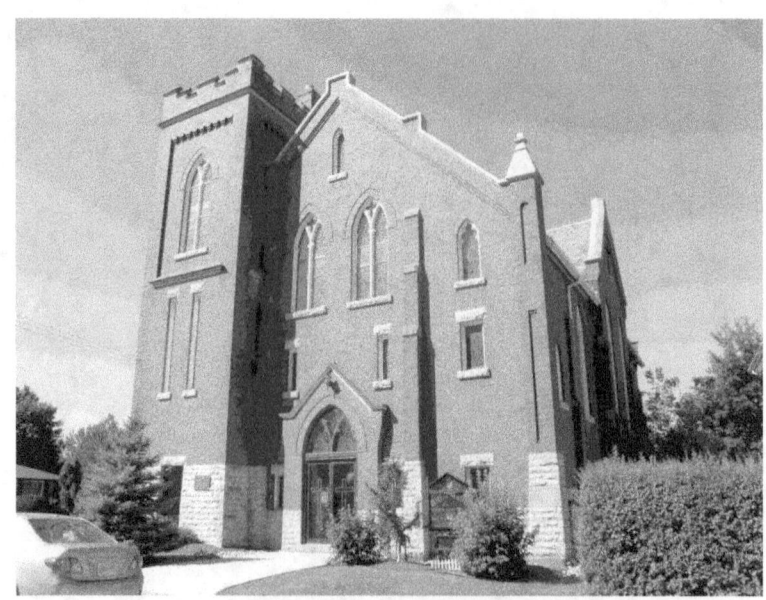

Presbyterian Church erected 1869, rebuilt 1915
Now Willis United Church

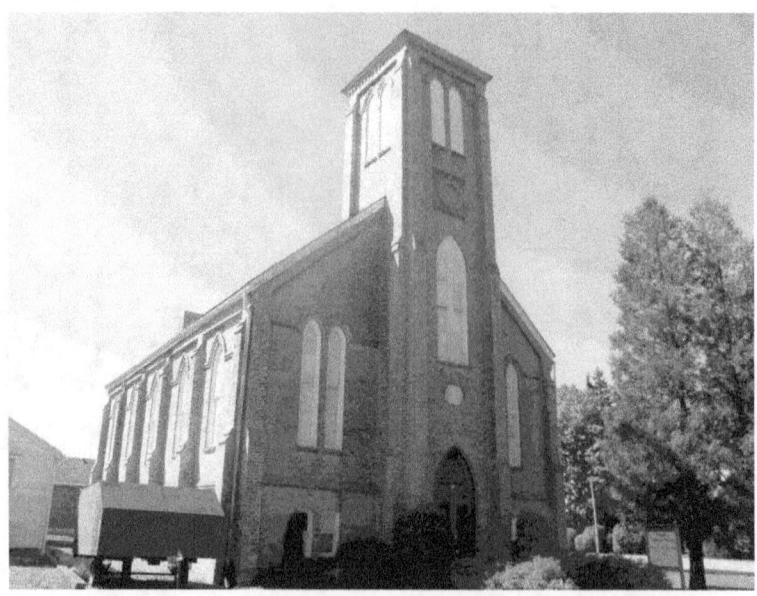

Drumbo Baptist Church, 20 Pinkham Street
Regular Baptist Church A.D. 1876

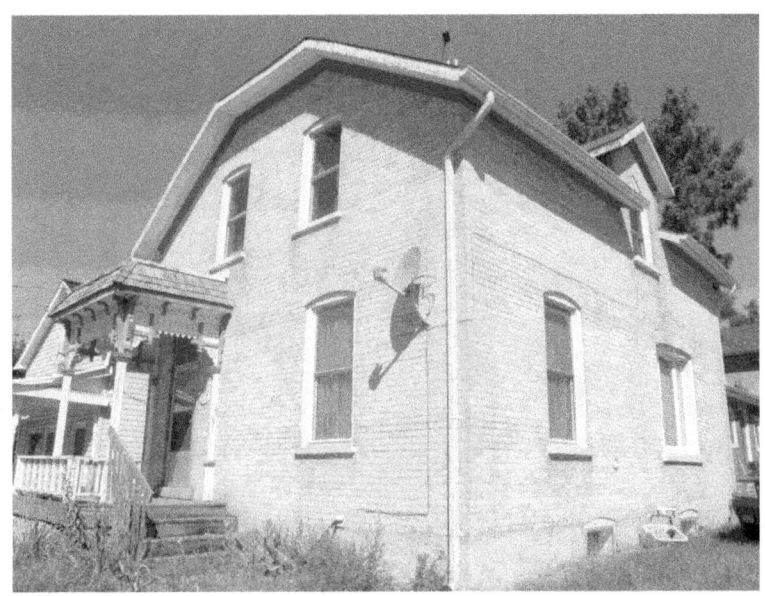

#25

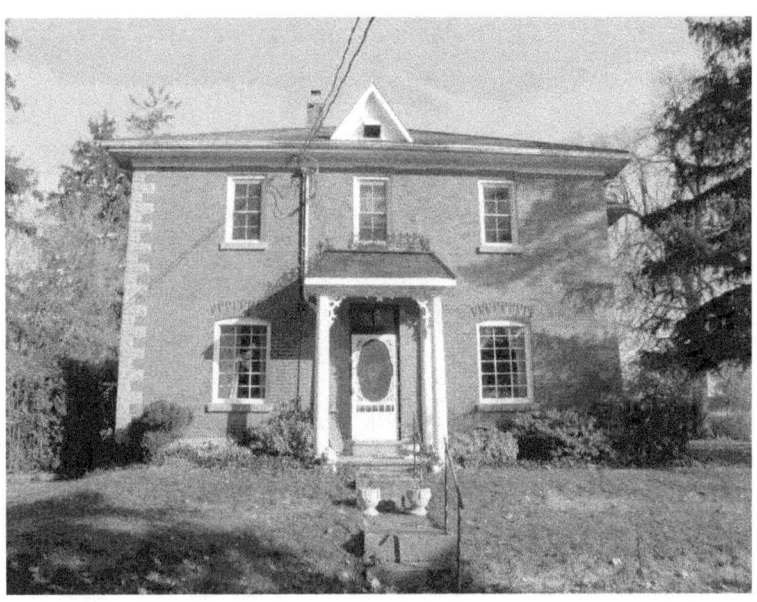

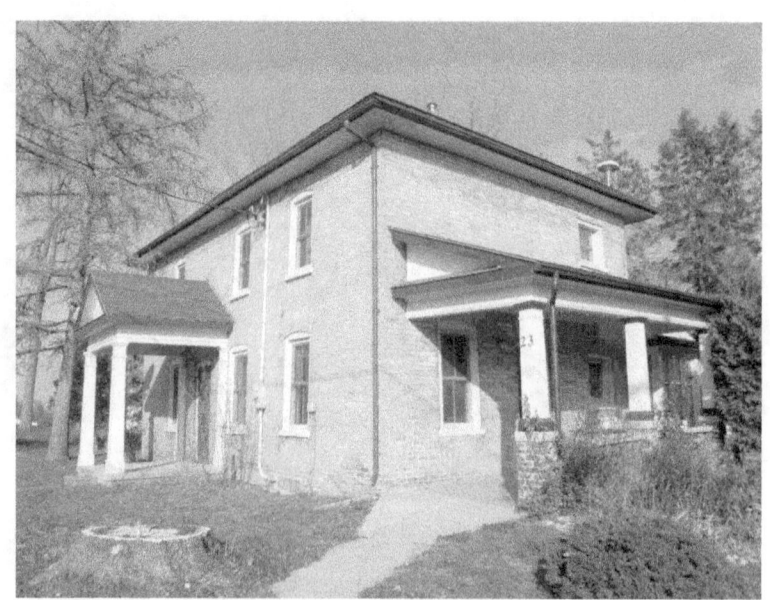

#23

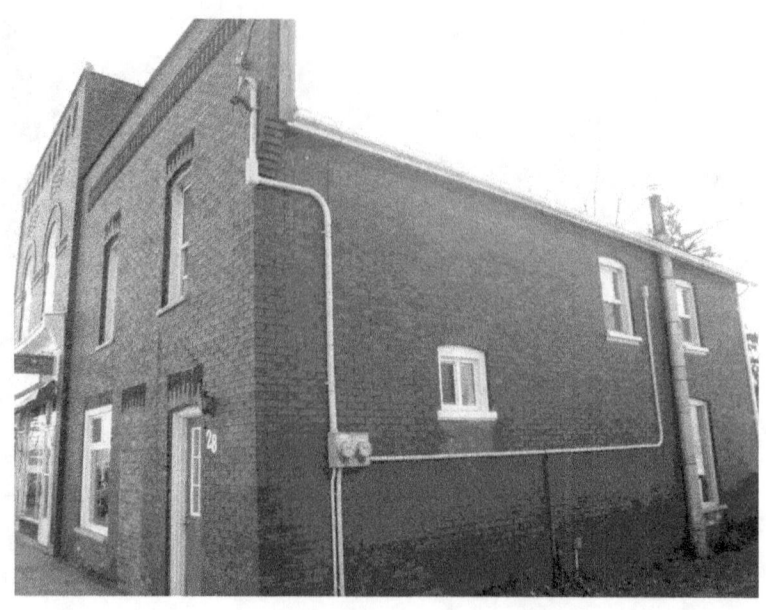

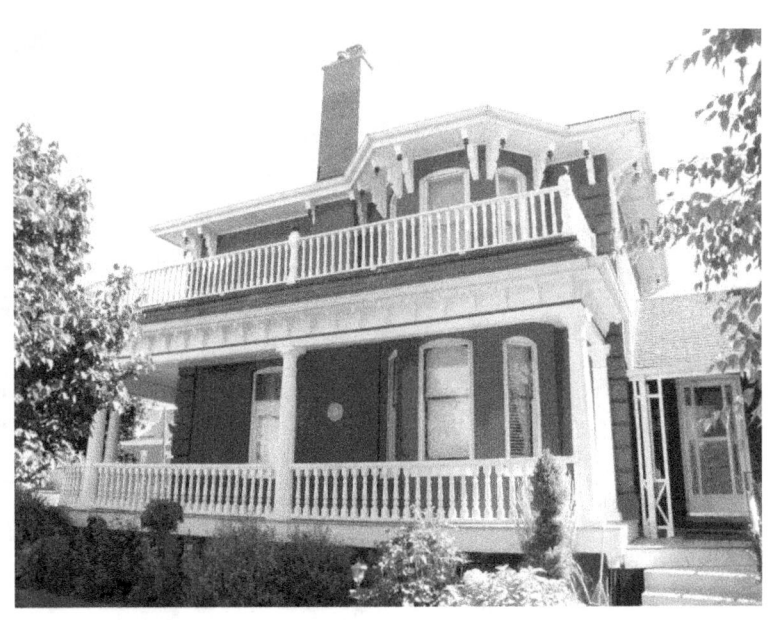

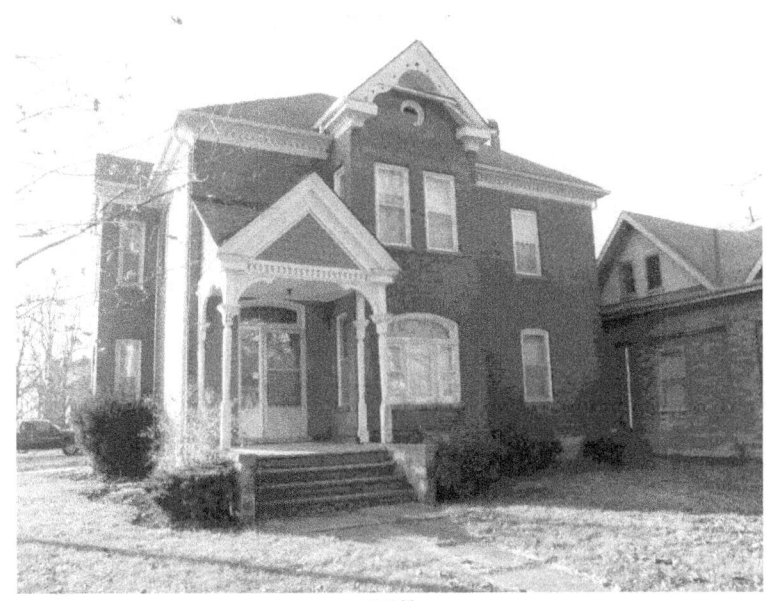

#15

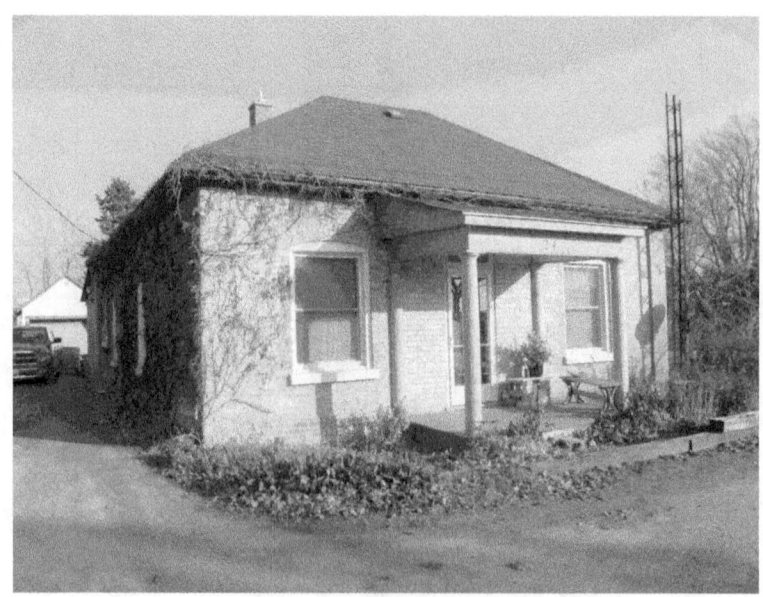

#24 – brick cottage

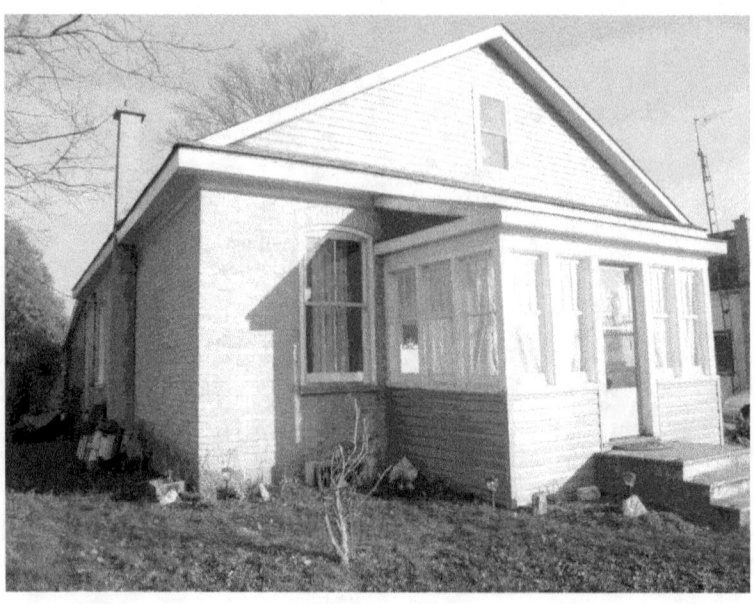

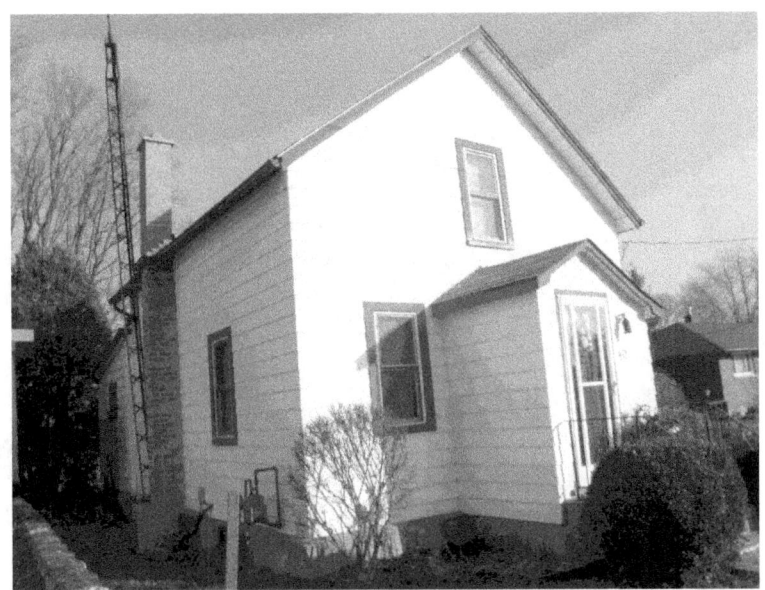

#40

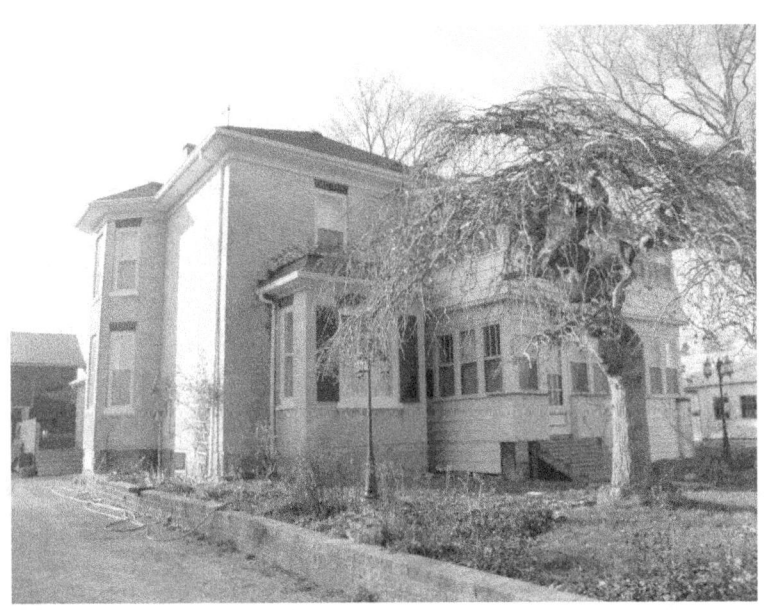

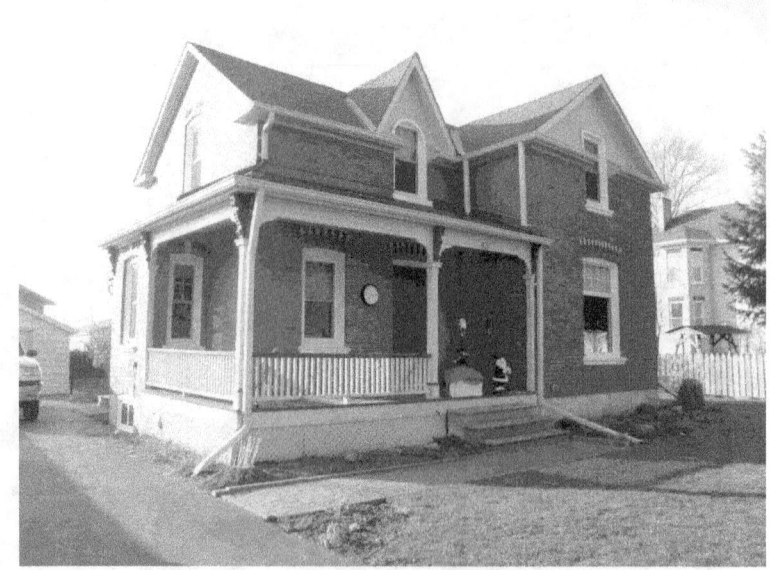

43 Oxford Street

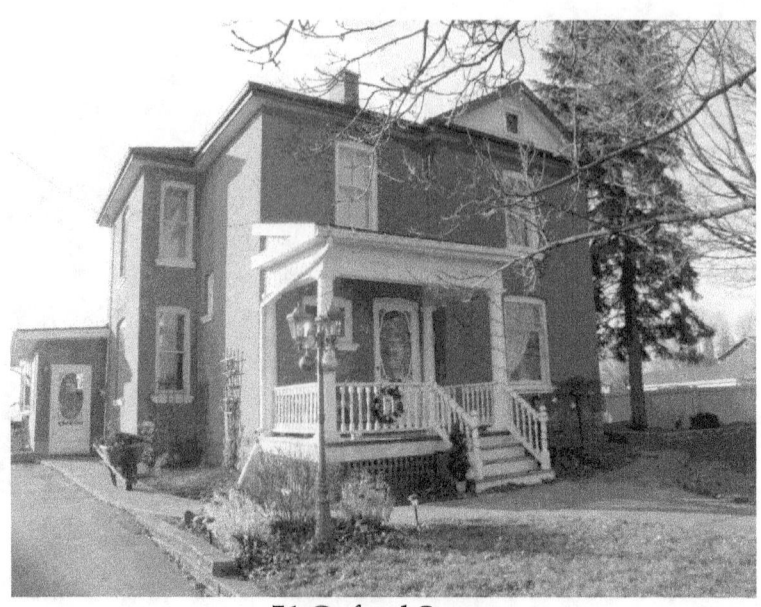

51 Oxford Street

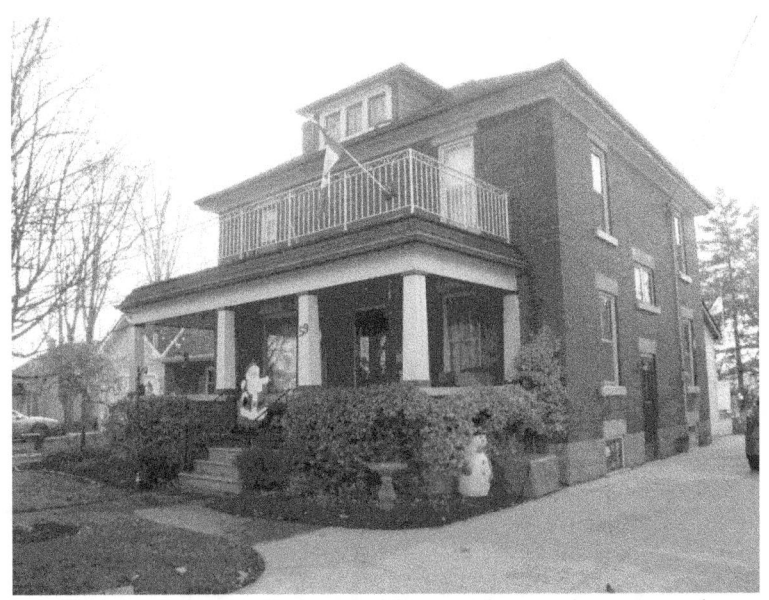

59 Oxford Street with balcony above the veranda
Dormer window above

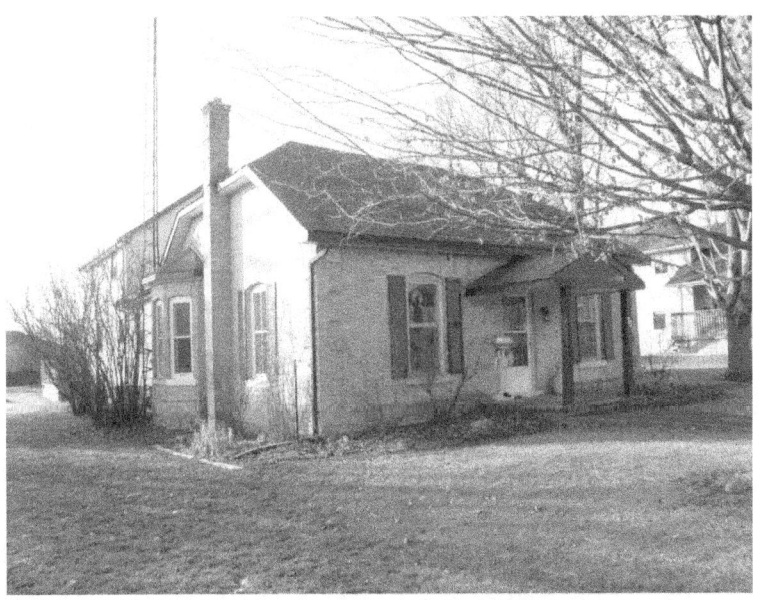

75 Oxford Street – brick cottage

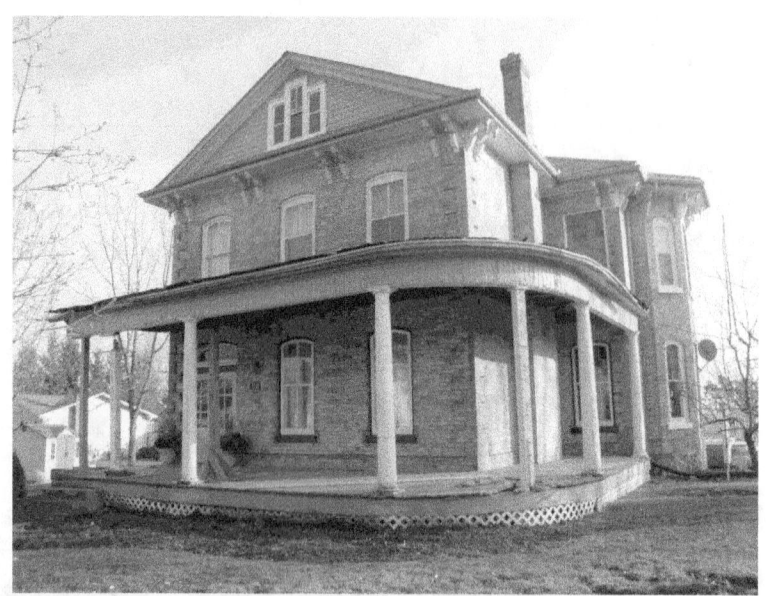

23 Oxford Street - Prominent brackets on the cornice (roof overhang), triangular pediment above with a Palladian type triple window in the tympanum with the centre window flanked by two lower windows

Princeton

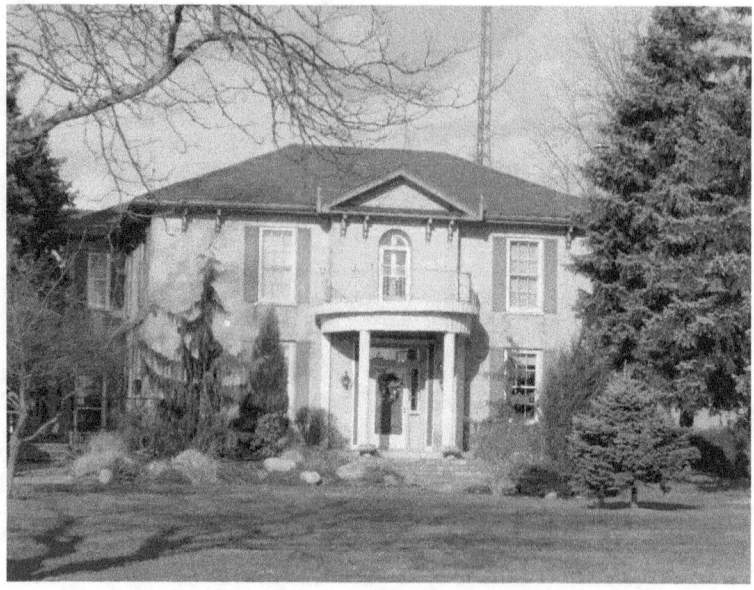

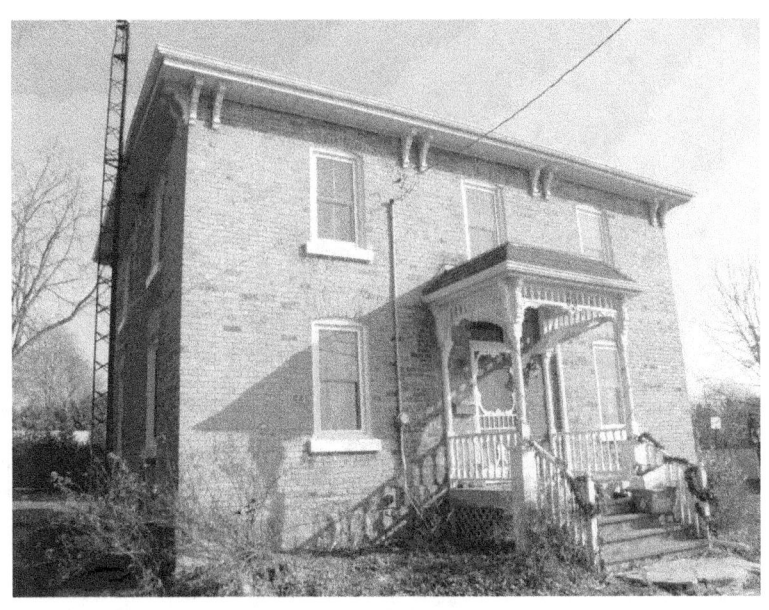

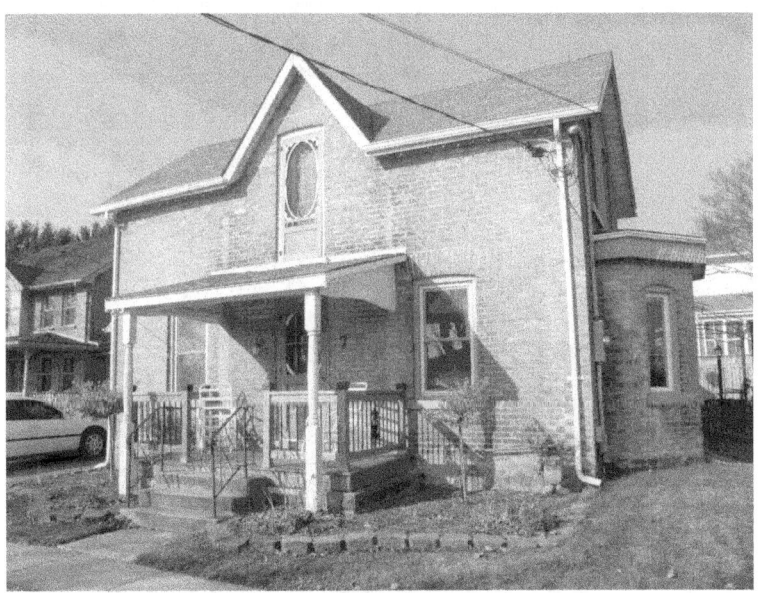

7 Elgin Street

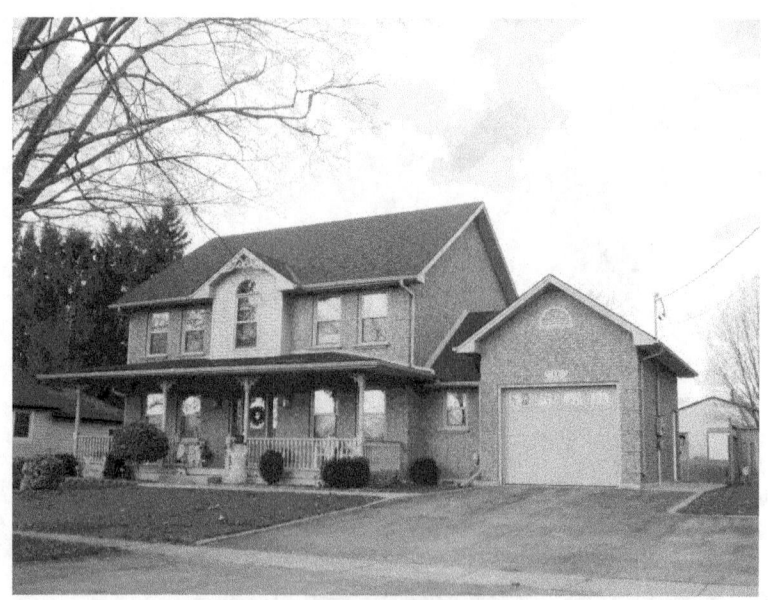

11 Elgin Street

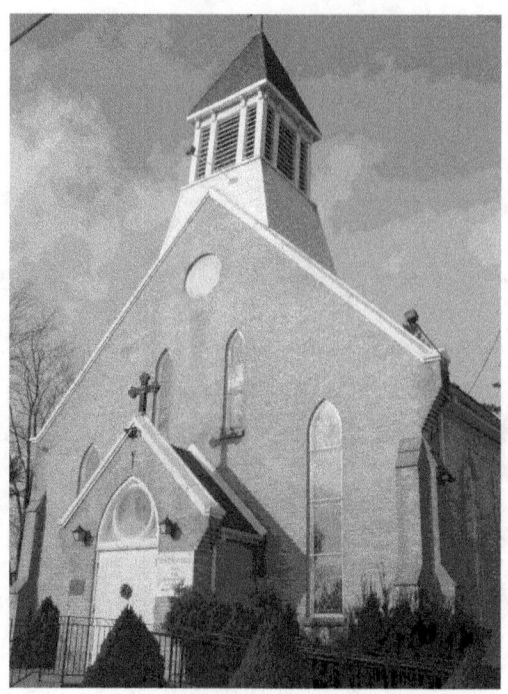

Sacred Heart Church established 1888

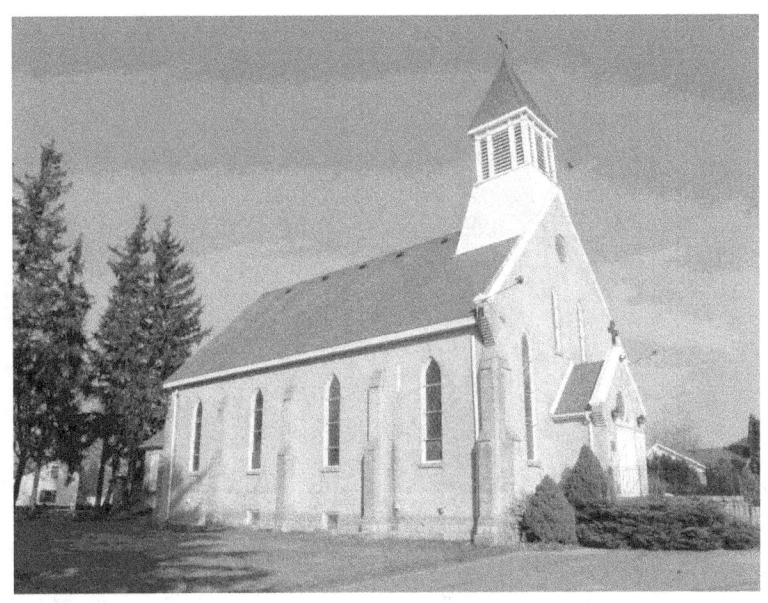

Sacred Heart Church

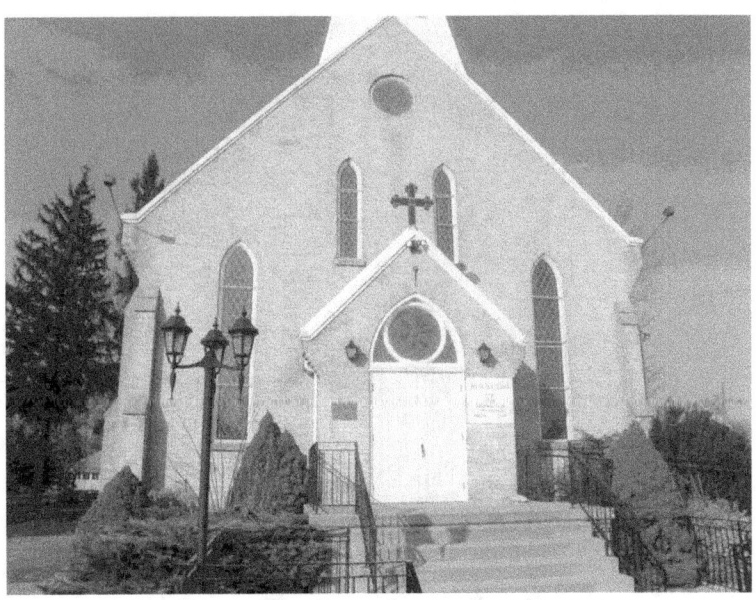

Rose window above the door

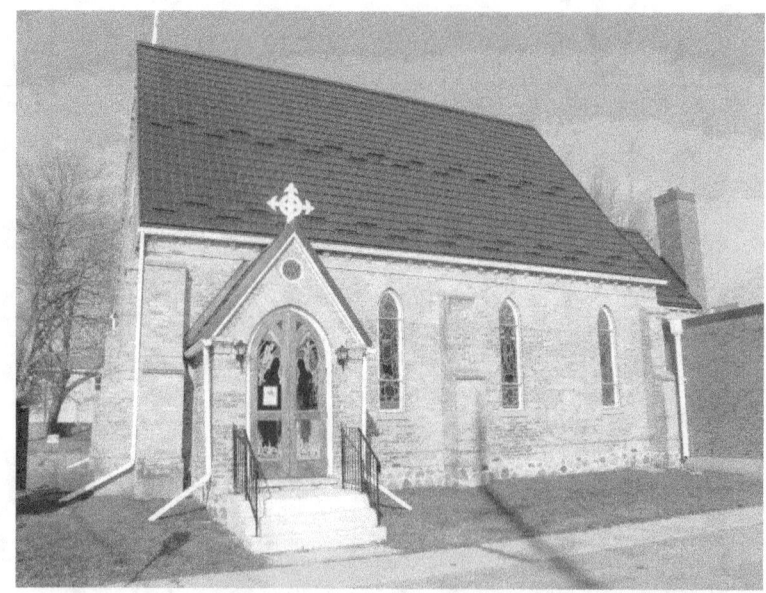

St. Paul's Anglican Church – built in 1867, restored 1917
4 Elgin Street East, corner of Main Street

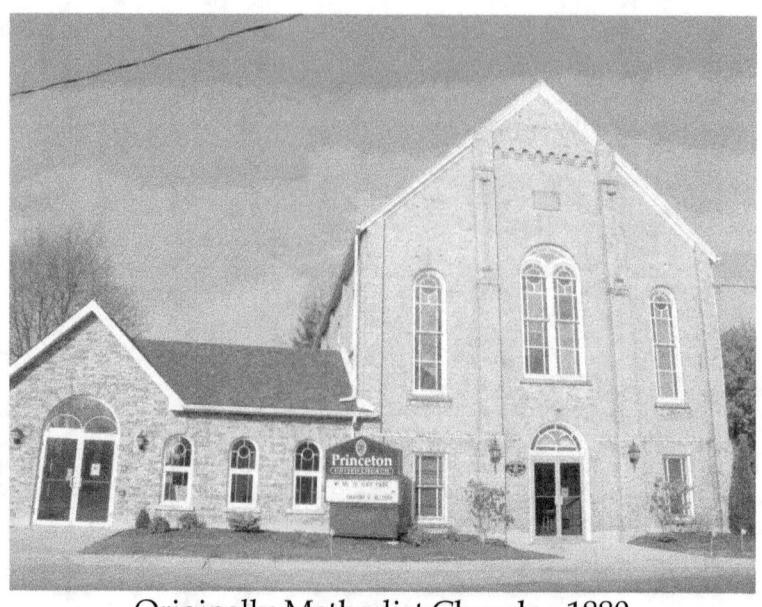

Originally Methodist Church – 1880
Now Princeton United Church – Elgin Street

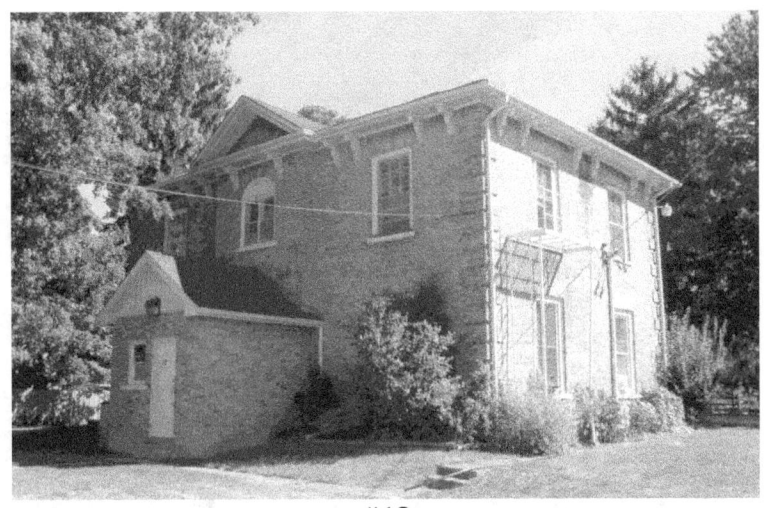

#12

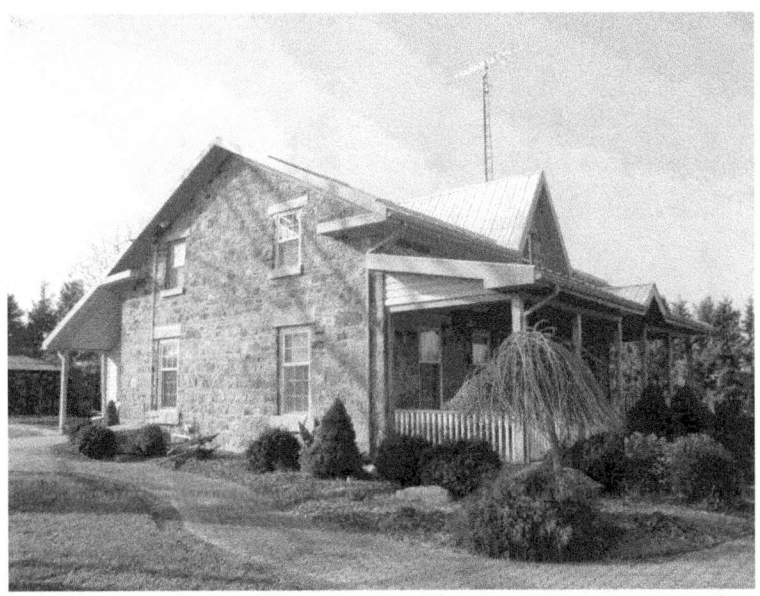

Stone house – Gothic Revival style with centre arch
Cornice return popular in Neo-classical Ontario architecture

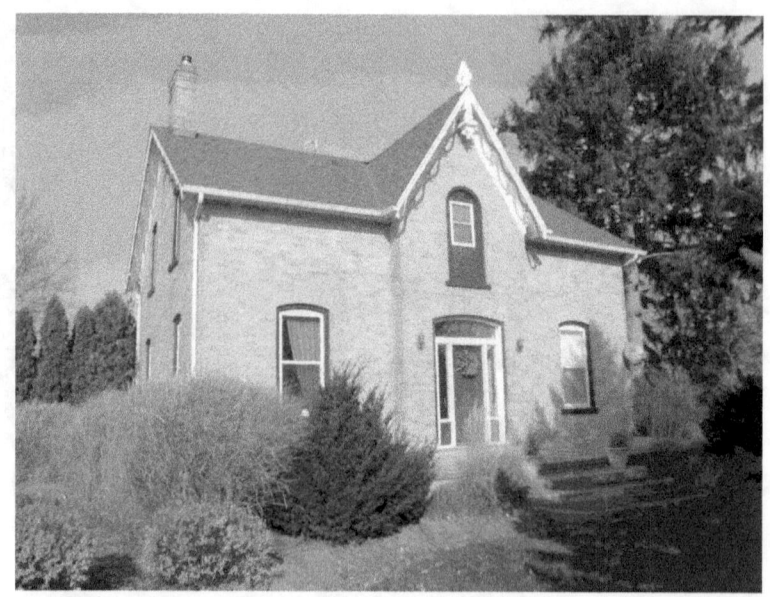

Gothic Revival style with gingerbread vergeboard

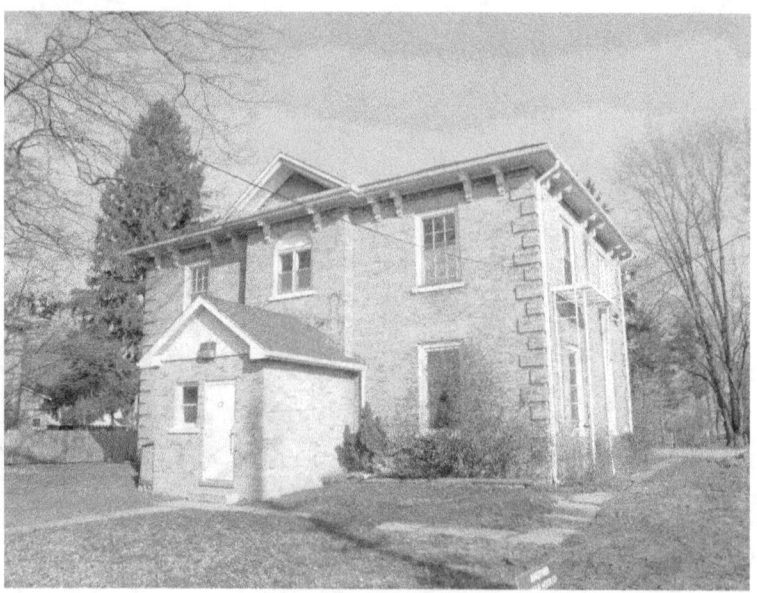

Cornice brackets

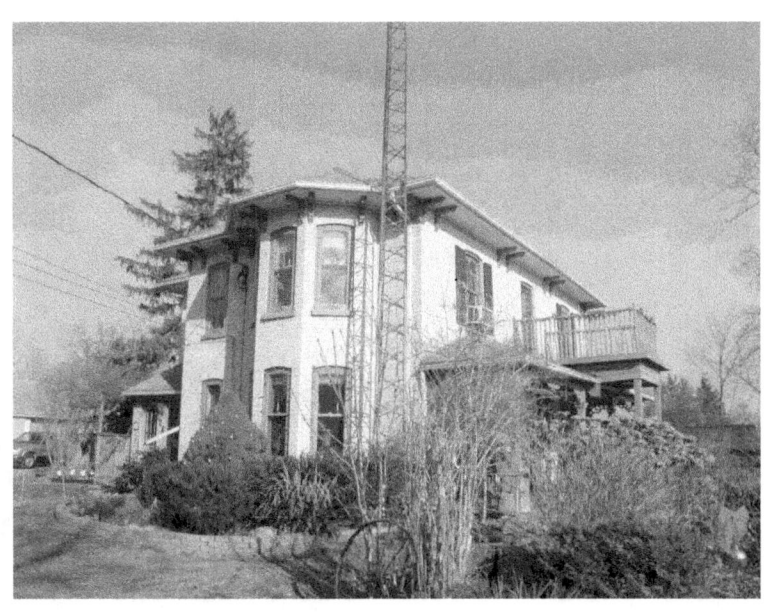

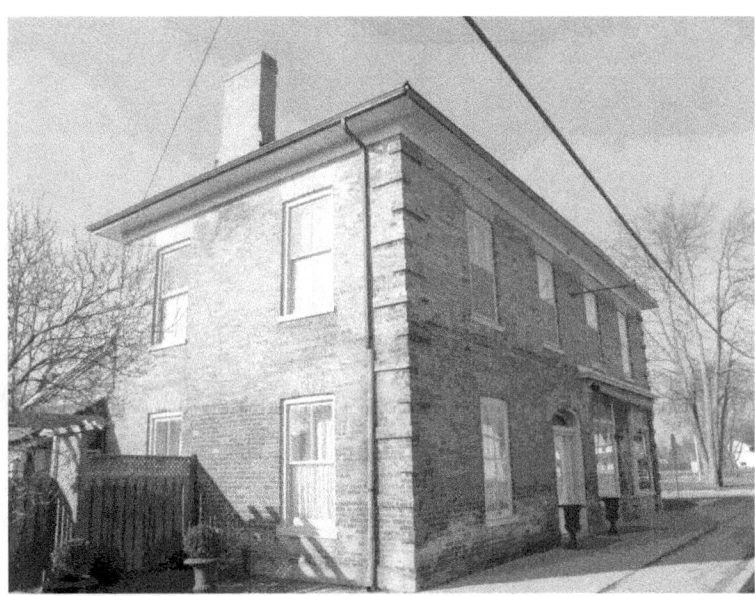

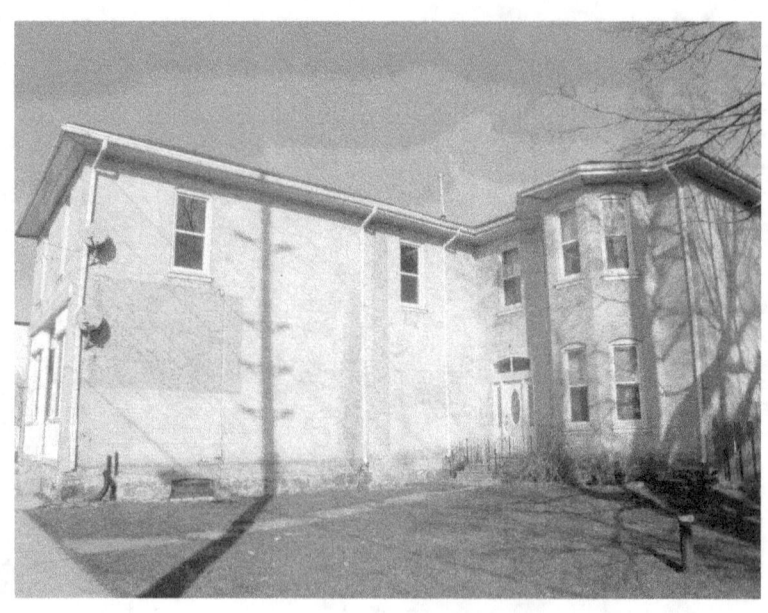

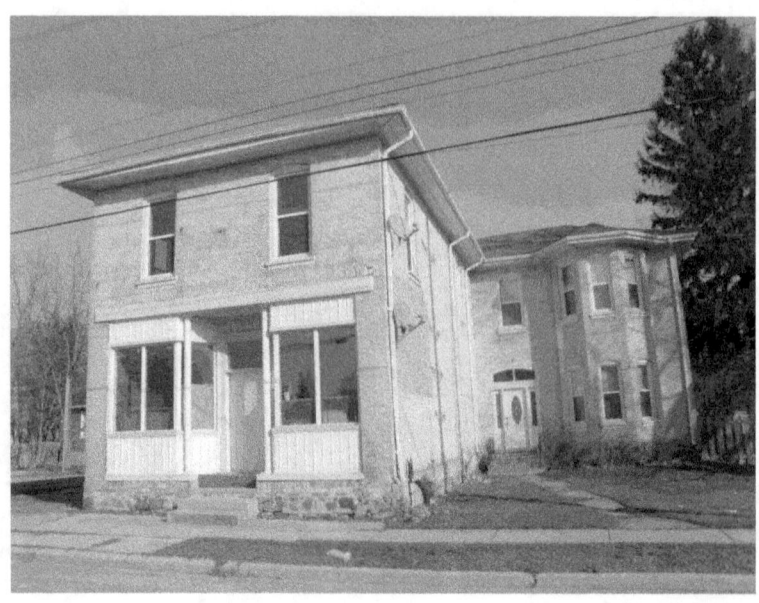

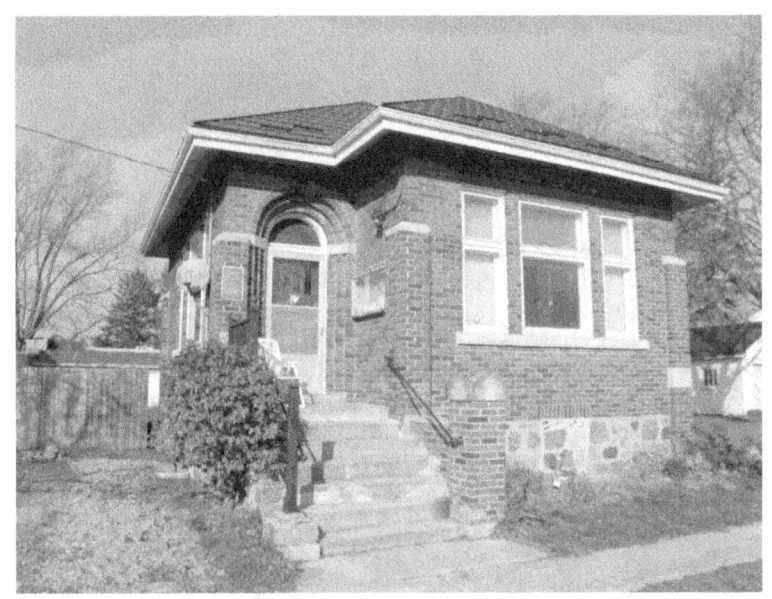

Branch of Oxford County Library plaque
House built in 1921

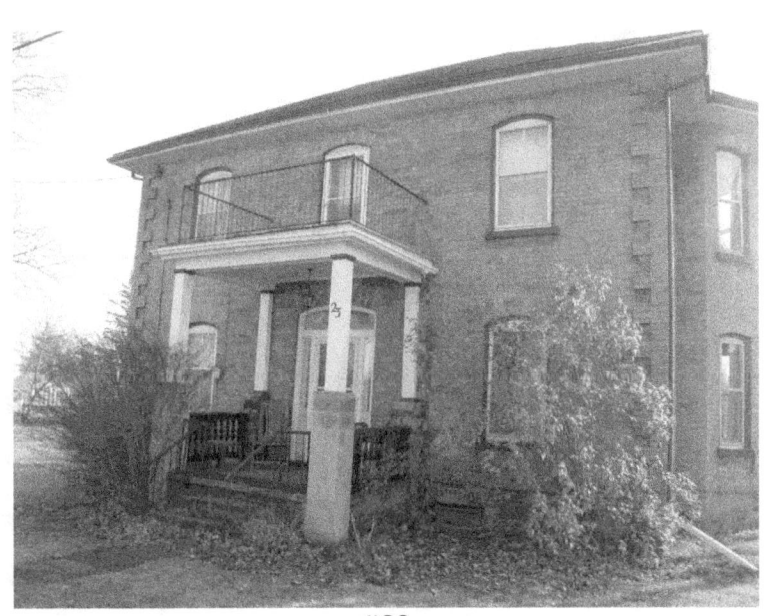

#23

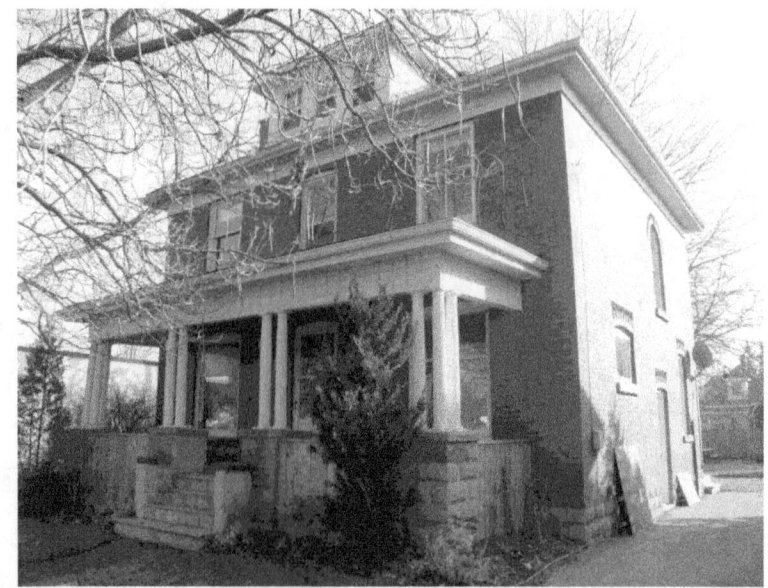

#20 with veranda on lower level, and a dormer extending out from the roof

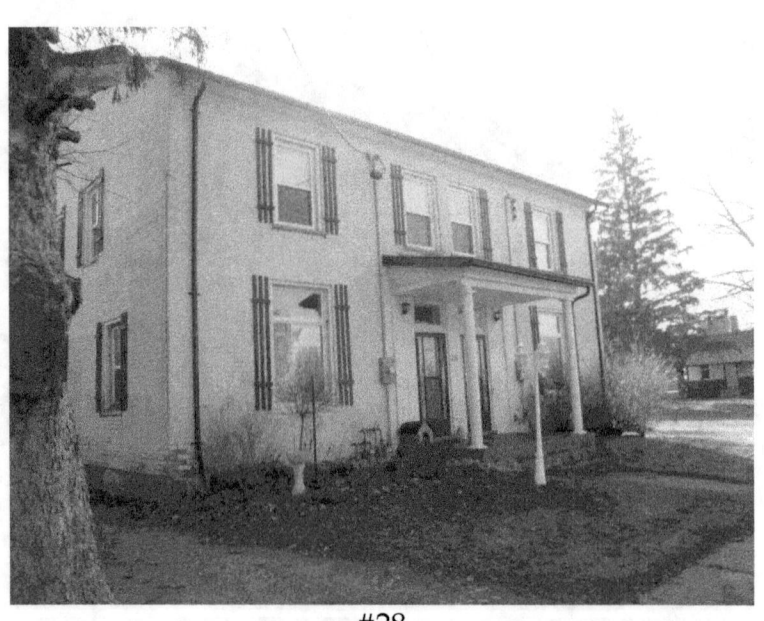

#28

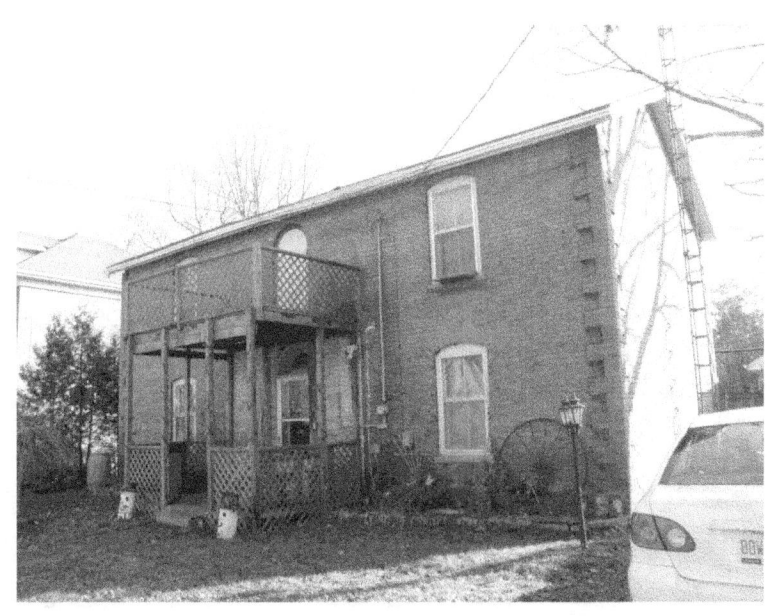

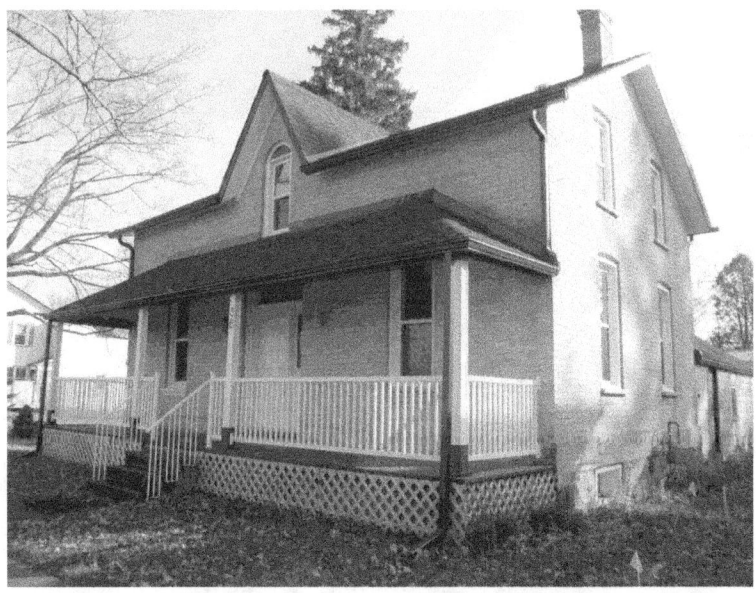

#36 – Gothic Revival style with small centre arch

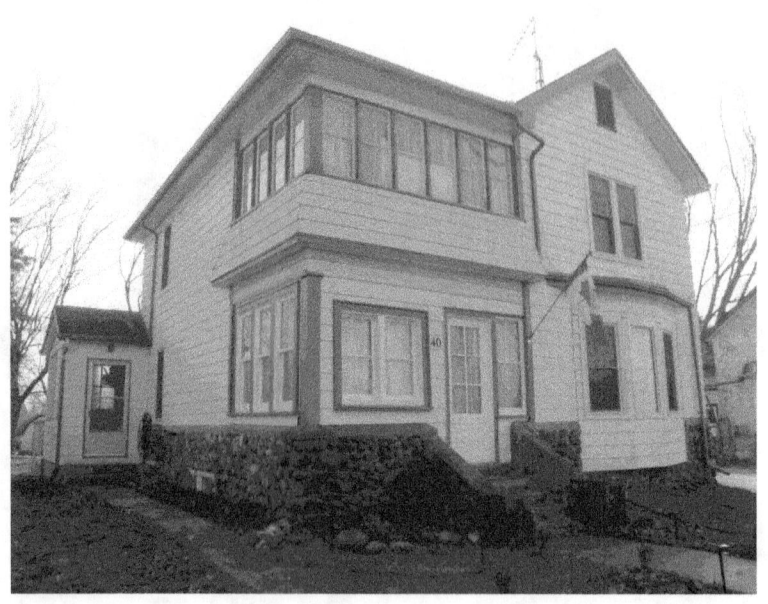

#40

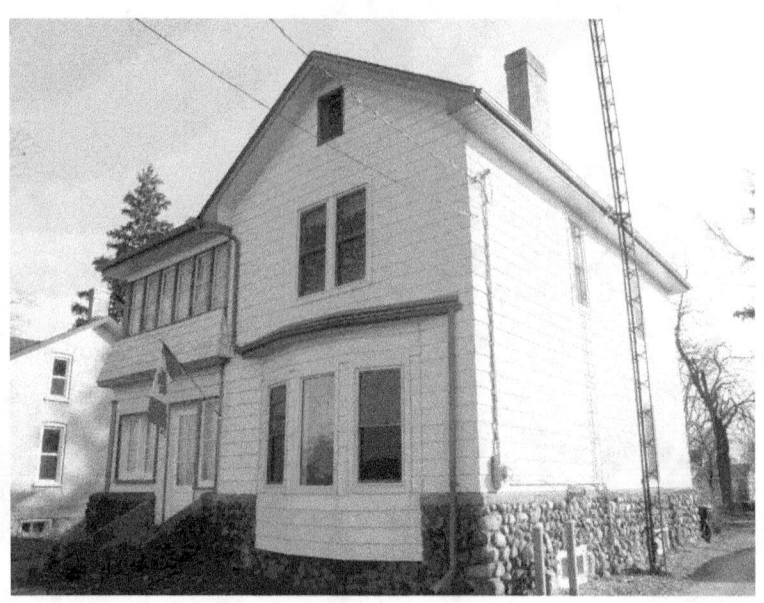

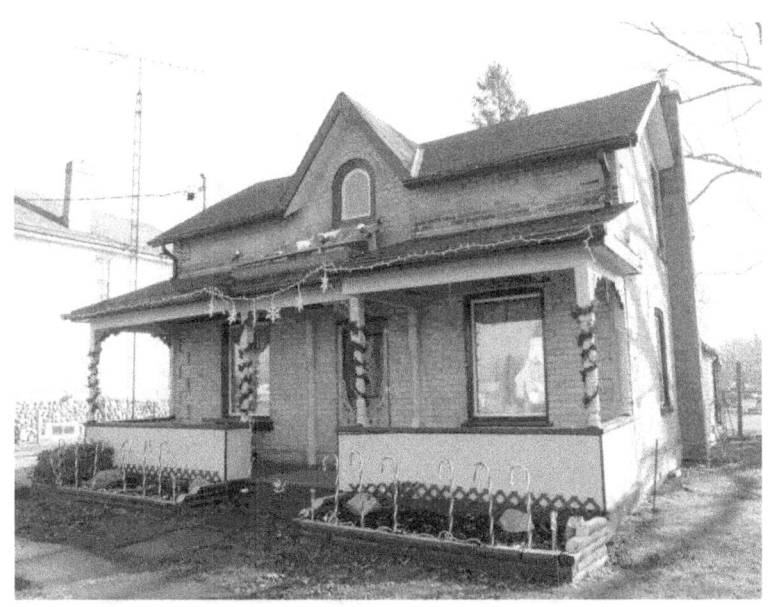

Both are Gothic Revival style cottages

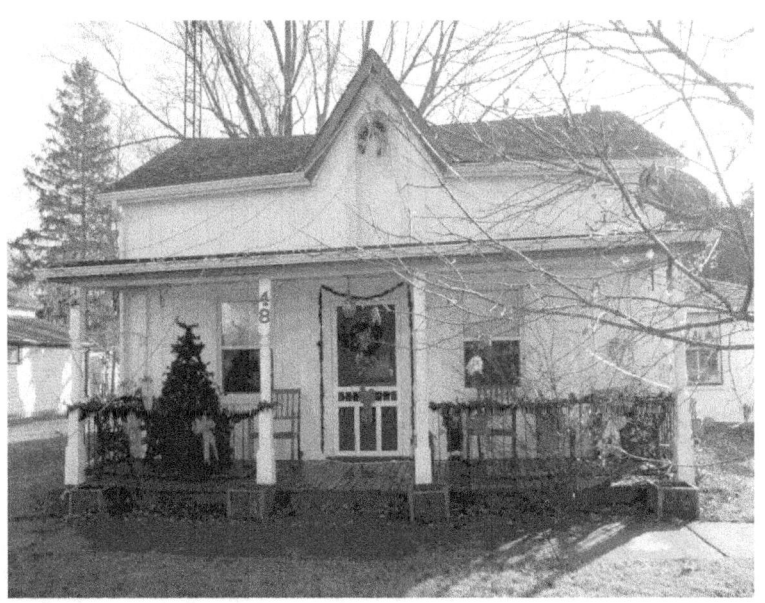

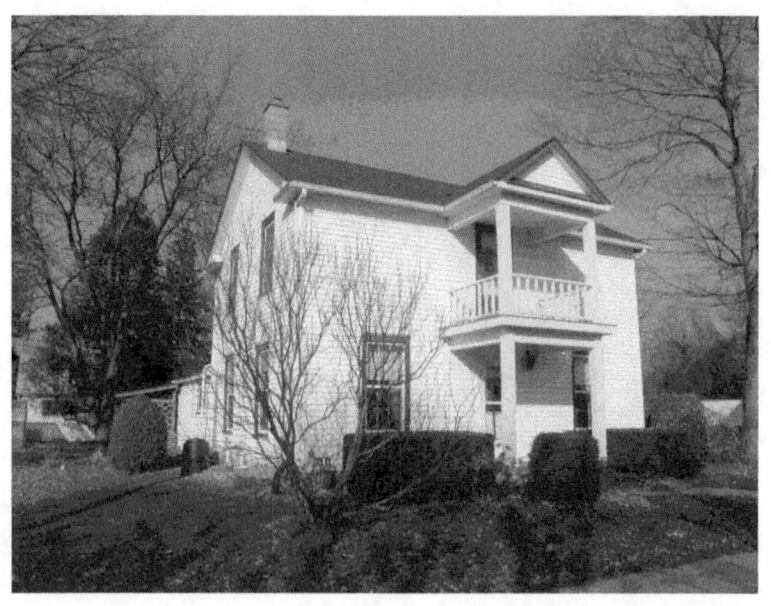

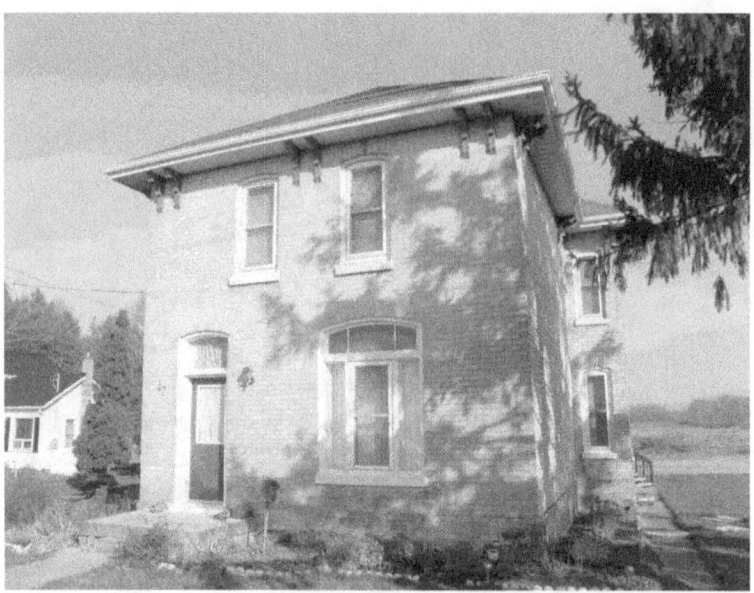

#47 – yellow brick with brick foundation

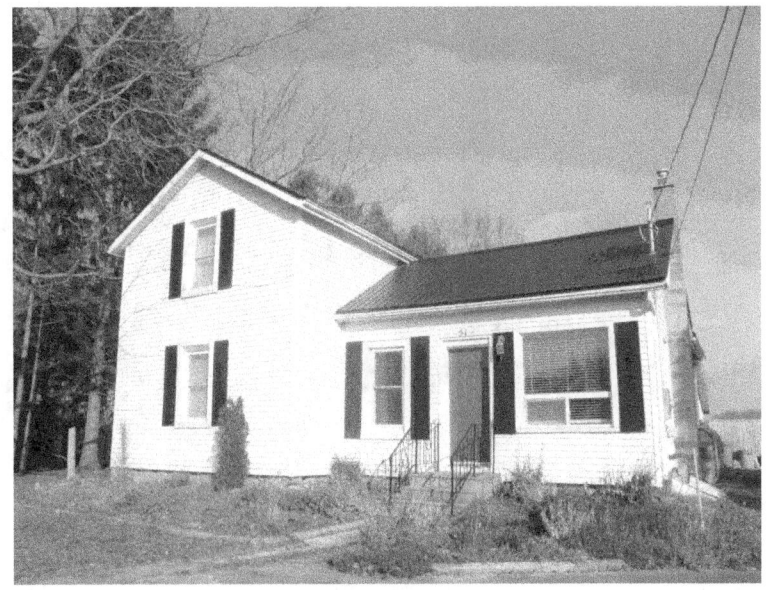

#51

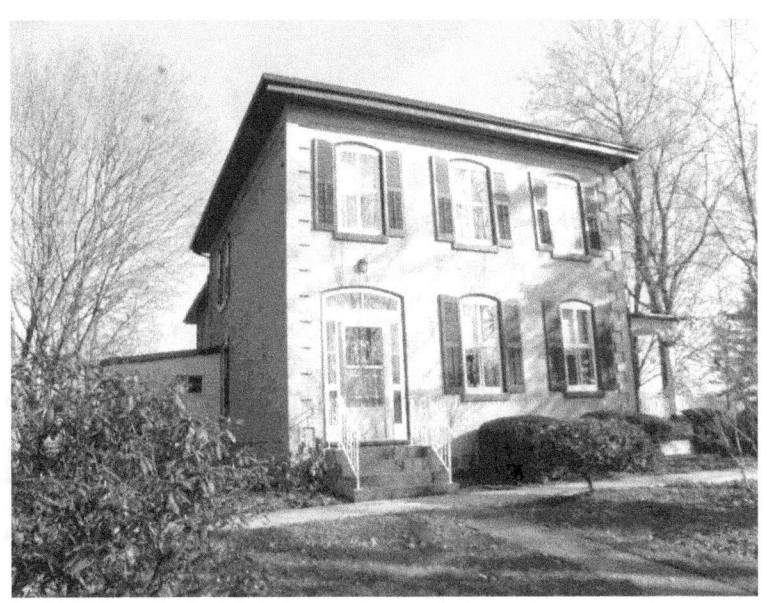

Georgian style

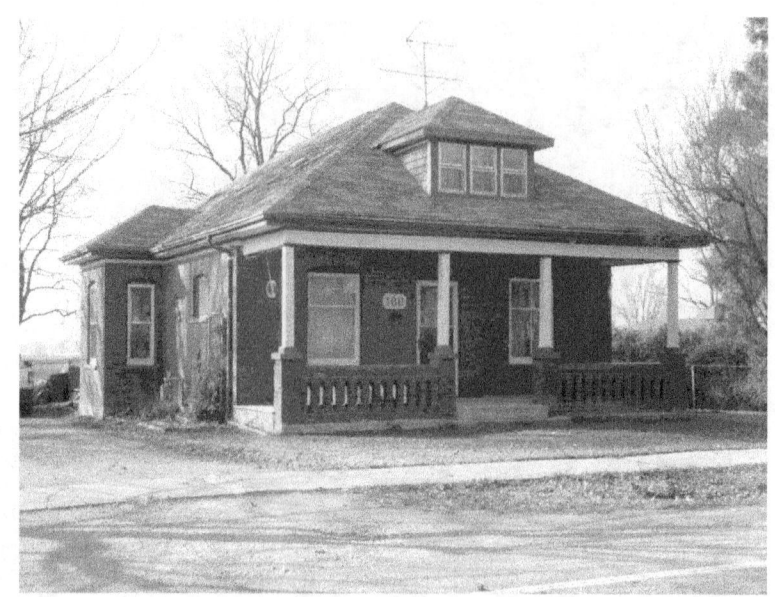

#100 – with dormer gable window extending out of the roof

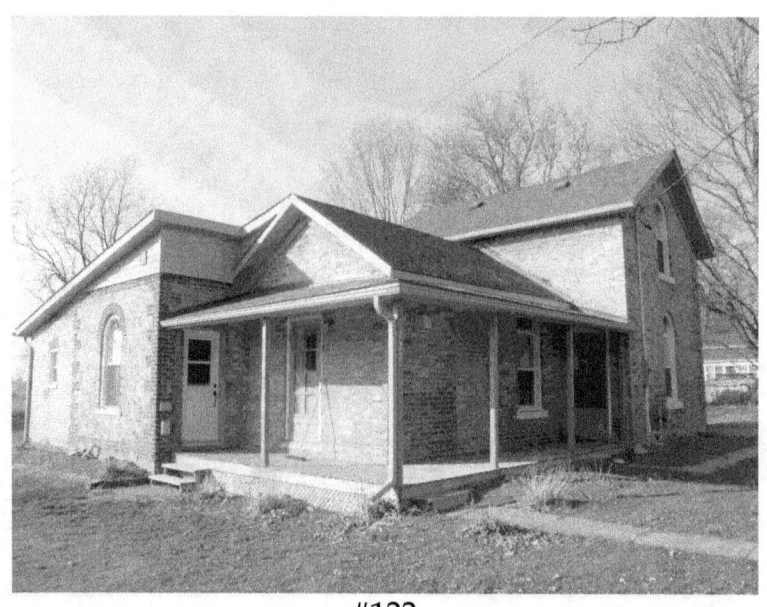

#122

Plattsville

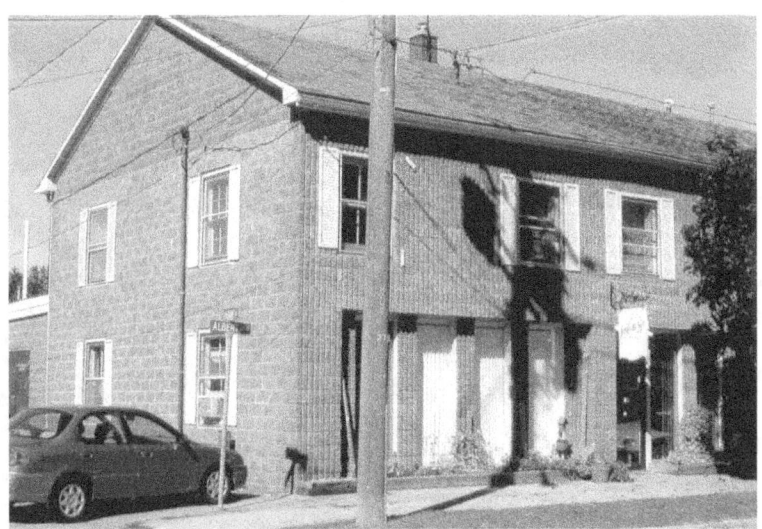

Forget-Me-Not – Albert and Hume Streets

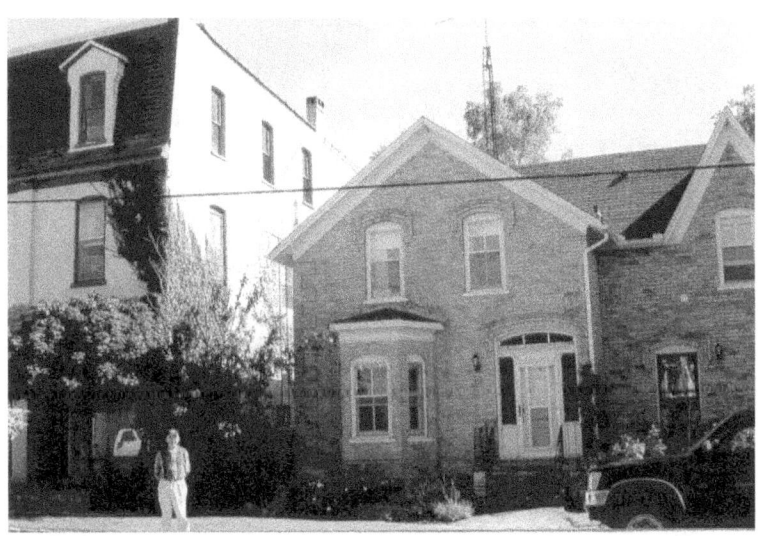

#70

Washington

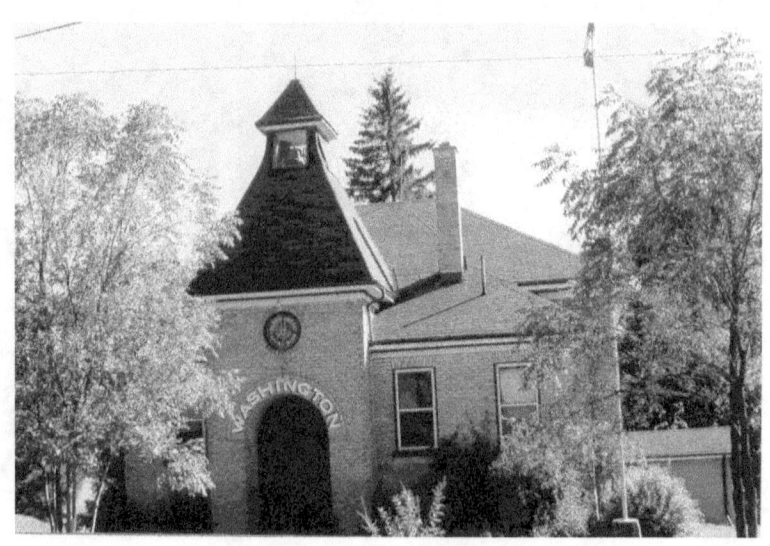

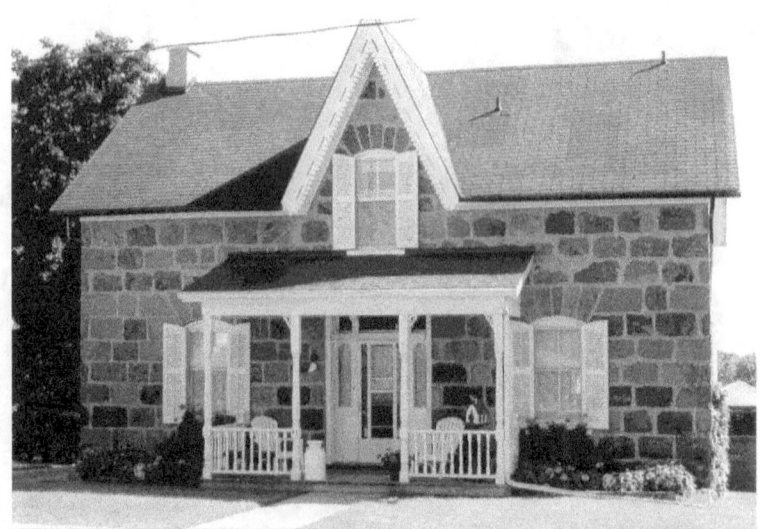

Gothic Revival stone cottage

Windfall

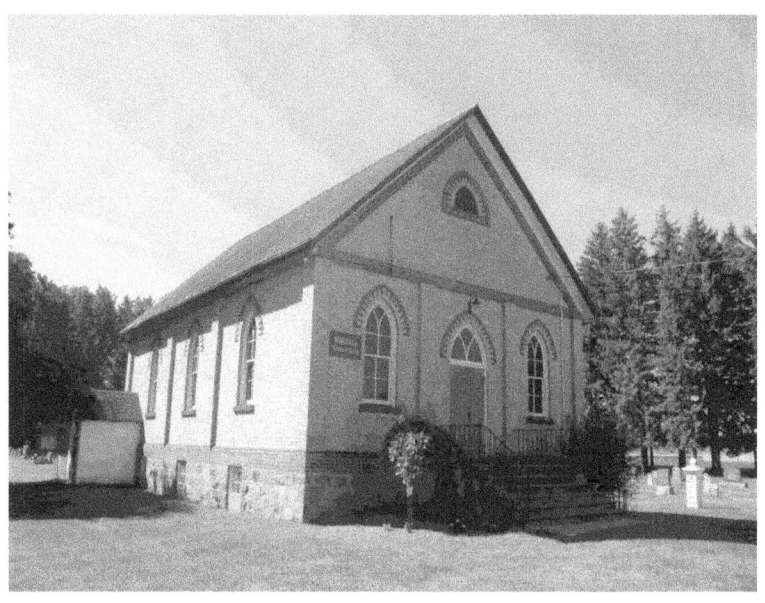

Windfall United Church – Oxford Road 29
Originally United Brethren Church erected in 1899

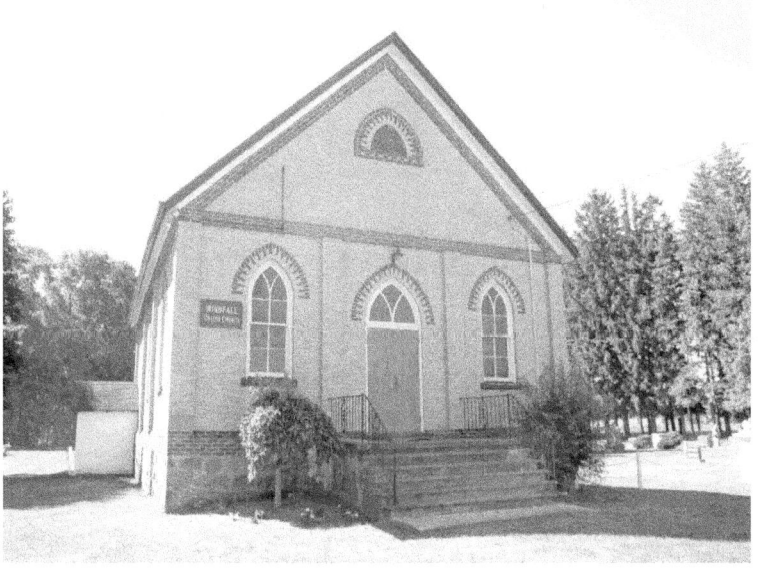

www.ingramcontent.com/pod-product-compliance
Lightning Source LLC
Chambersburg PA
CBHW051305170526
45165CB00004B/1866